What kind of animal is it?

Many Kinds of Animals

Molly Aloian & Bobbie Kalman

🌿 Crabtree Publishing Company

www.crabtreebooks.com

Many Kinds of Animals

Created by Bobbie Kalman

Dedicated by John Siemens
To Erika, Matthew, and Katherine, my kind of animals.

Editor-in-Chief
Bobbie Kalman

Writing team
Molly Aloian
Bobbie Kalman

Substantive editor
Kathryn Smithyman

Editors
Robin Johnson
Kelley MacAulay
Reagan Miller

Design
Katherine Berti
Robert MacGregor (series logo)

Production coordinator
Katherine Berti

Photo research
Crystal Sikkens

Consultant
Patricia Loesche, Ph.D., Animal Behavior Program,
Department of Psychology, University of Washington

Illustrations
Barbara Bedell: pages 4 (all except frog), 6 (top-left and right),
    9 (slug), 10 (top-left and right), 12, 17 (all except bristle worm),
    20 (millipede), 22 (sea horse), 26, 27, 29 (bottom), 30,
    32 (all except amphibians and mammals)
Anne Giffard: page 15
Katherine Berti: pages 5 (snake), 10 (snake), 29 (top)
Cori Marvin: page 14
Jeannette McNaughton-Julich: page 28 (top-left and right)
Margaret Amy Salter: pages 5 (all except snake), 6 (snail), 8,
    9 (octopus), 18, 19, 20 (all except millipede), 21, 22 (fish)
Bonna Rouse: pages 7, 11, 16, 17 (bristle worm), 24, 25, 28 (bottom),
    32 (amphibians and mammals)
Tiffany Wybouw: page 4 (frog)

Images by Bobbie Kalman: page 28; Adobe Image Library, Brand X
    Pictures, Corbis, Corel, Creatas, Digital Stock, Digital Vision,
    Eyewire, Otto Rogge Photography, and Photodisc

Crabtree Publishing Company

www.crabtreebooks.com   1-800-387-7650

Copyright © **2005 CRABTREE PUBLISHING COMPANY.**
All rights reserved. No part of this publication may be reproduced,
stored in a retrieval system or be transmitted in any form or by any
means, electronic, mechanical, photocopying, recording, or otherwise,
without the prior written permission of Crabtree Publishing Company.
In Canada: We acknowledge the financial support of the Government
of Canada through the Canada Book Fund for our publishing activities.

Printed in Canada/042013/MA20130325

Library of Congress Cataloging-in-Publication Data
Aloian, Molly.
  Many kinds of animals / Molly Aloian & Bobbie Kalman.
      p. cm. -- (What kind of animal is it?)
  Includes index.
  ISBN-13: 978-0-7787-2156-7 (RLB)
  ISBN-10: 0-7787-2156-6 (RLB)
  ISBN-13: 978-0-7787-2214-4 (pbk.)
  ISBN-10: 0-7787-2214-7 (pbk.)
  1. Animals--Juvenile literature. I. Kalman, Bobbie. II. Title. III. Series.
  QL49.A445 2005
  590--dc22
                                                    2005000503
                                                         LC

Published in Canada
Crabtree Publishing
616 Welland Ave.
St. Catharines, ON
L2M 5V6

Published in the United States
Crabtree Publishing
PMB 59051
350 Fifth Avenue, 59th Floor
New York, New York 10118

Published in the United Kingdom
Crabtree Publishing
Maritime House
Basin Road North, Hove
BN41 1WR

Published in Australia
Crabtree Publishing
3 Charles Street
Coburg North
VIC, 3058

Contents

What are animals?   4

Animal coverings   6

Backbones   8

Cold or warm blood?   10

Where do animals live?   12

On the move   14

Sponges, starfish, and corals   16

Worms   17

Mollusks   18

Animals called arthropods   20

Many kinds of fish   22

Amphibians   24

Reptiles   26

Beautiful birds   28

Mammals   30

Words to know and Index   32

What are animals?

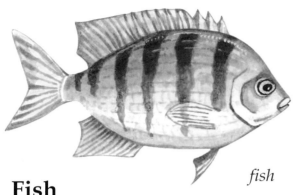

fish

Fish
Fish are one group
of animals.

Animals are living things. They are found all over the world. Some animals live in water, and others live on land. There are many groups of animals. Some of the groups are shown on these pages. How many of these animals do you know?

snail

Mollusks
Snails belong to a group of animals called **mollusks**.

Amphibians
Amphibians are another group of animals. Frogs are amphibians.

frog

worm

Worms
Worms make up a group of animals. There are many kinds of worms.

spider

Arthropods
Arthropods are a group of animals that includes spiders.

4

snake

Reptiles
Snakes belong to a group of animals called **reptiles**.

bird

Birds
Birds make up their own group of animals.

cat

bear

Mammals
One group of animals is called **mammals**. Bears and cats are mammals. People are mammals, too.

Animal coverings

A snake is a reptile. Snakes have scales on their bodies.

Different animals have different coverings on their bodies. Mammals have fur or hair. Reptiles are covered in **scales**. Birds are covered in feathers. Arthropods are covered in **exoskeletons**.

scales

exoskeleton

A beetle is an arthropod. Beetles have exoskeletons. Exoskeletons are hard cases.

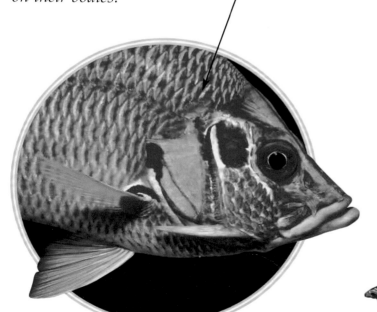

Most fish are also covered in scales.

A snail is a mollusk. Snails have hard shells covering their bodies.

Birds have feathers on their bodies. Feathers help birds fly.

People are mammals. People have hair.

This dog is a mammal. Dogs are covered in fur.

A salamander is an amphibian. Salamanders have smooth, slimy skin.

Backbones

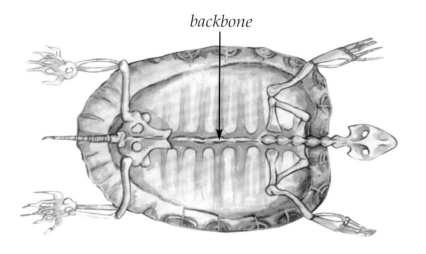

backbone

A tortoise's backbone is inside its body.

Some animals have **backbones** inside their bodies. A backbone is a group of bones in the middle of an animal's back. People have backbones, too!

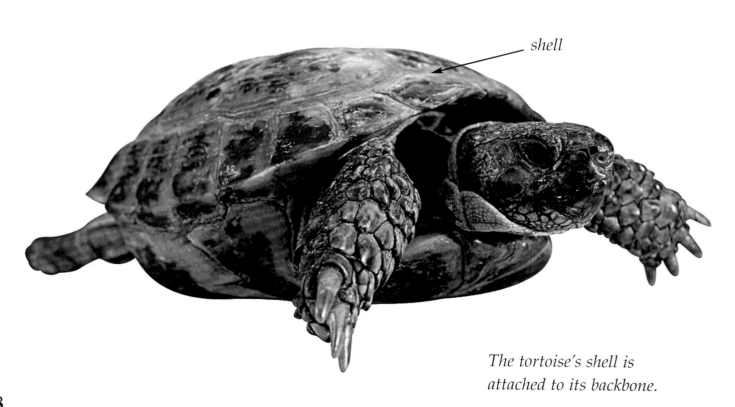

shell

The tortoise's shell is attached to its backbone.

No backbones

Most of the animals on Earth do not have backbones. In fact, they do not have any bones at all!

Jellyfish do not have backbones.

Millipedes do not have backbones.

Slugs do not have backbones.

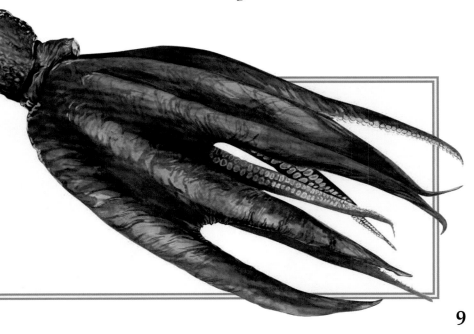

Soft bodies

Many animals without backbones have soft bodies. Octopuses have soft bodies. An octopus is a mollusk.

Cold or warm blood?

Reptiles are cold-blooded animals.

Most animals are **cold-blooded**. The body temperature of a cold-blooded animal does not stay the same. It changes. When the weather is warm, the animal's body is warm. When the weather is cold, the animal's body is cold. If a cold-blooded animal needs to warm up, it sits in the sun.

This bullfrog is a cold-blooded amphibian. It is sitting in the sun to warm its body.

Warm blood

Warm-blooded animals have warm bodies. Their body temperatures do not change much. They stay about the same, even when the animals are in cold places. Mammals such as bears are warm-blooded animals. People are also warm-blooded.

Birds are warm-blooded animals. A parrot is a kind of bird.

Where do animals live?

Different animals live in different **habitats**. A habitat is the natural place where an animal lives. Forests, deserts, and fields are animal habitats. Some animals even live in freezing cold places!

Cold and icy

The penguins shown left are birds. They live in Antarctica. Antarctica is a place that is always cold. Most of Antarctica is covered with snow and ice. Penguins live on the ice and swim in the cold water.

Many lizards live in hot deserts. Deserts are habitats that get very little rain.

Raccoons live in forests.
This raccoon's home is in a tree.

Living in water

Fish and many other kinds of animals live in water. Most of the animals that live in water can swim. Some animals that live on land are also able to swim. Name three land animals that can swim. Are you a swimmer?

Sea otters live in water.

On the move

Animals move from place to place in different ways. Some animals walk or run. Some jump. Some animals fly, and some swim. Look at how these animals are moving. How do you move in water? How do you move up a hill?

A butterfly flies by flapping its wings.

Horses walk or run. They can also swim and jump.

14

Most birds can fly. This osprey flies from place to place looking for food.

A snake **slithers**. To slither means to slide on the belly.

On land, a tiger walks or runs. In water, a tiger swims.

A kangaroo jumps. It has strong back legs for jumping.

A grasshopper is another animal that jumps.

Sponges, starfish, and corals

Sponges, starfish, and corals do not look like animals, but they are animals! These animals do not have heads or brains. Sponges, starfish, and corals live in oceans.

A starfish has a simple body.
It has five arms that all look the same.

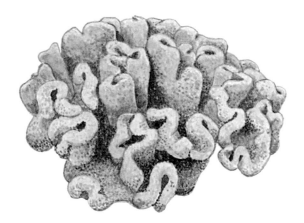

Corals come in different colors.
They can be pink, orange, or green.

This tube sponge looks like a plant,
but it is an animal.

Worms

There are many kinds of worms. Some worms live under the ground. Other worms live in oceans. Worms that live under the ground have soft, long, thin bodies. Some of the worms that live in oceans look like Christmas trees!

Christmas tree worms live in oceans.

*Bristle worms live in oceans, too. They have tiny hairs called **bristles** on their bodies.*

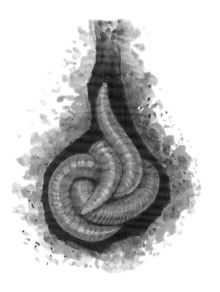

*Earthworms live in the ground. This earthworm is in a **burrow**. A burrow is an underground home.*

17

Mollusks

Mollusks are animals with soft bodies. They do not have backbones. Most mollusks have shells. Some mollusks live on land. Other mollusks live in water. The flame scallop, shown below, is a mollusk that lives in water.

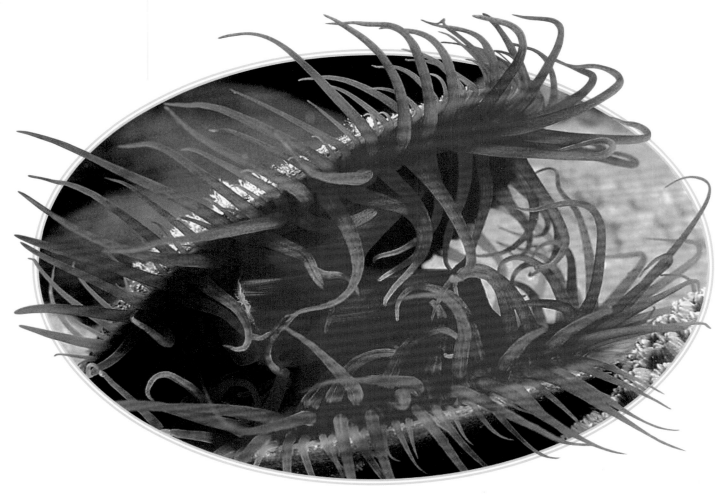

A clam has two shells that protect its soft body.

A snail is a mollusk with a shell.

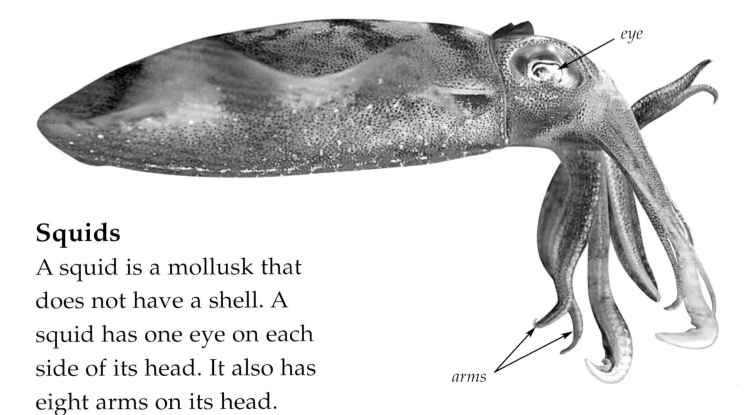

Squids

A squid is a mollusk that does not have a shell. A squid has one eye on each side of its head. It also has eight arms on its head.

Animals called arthropods

There are millions of arthropods on Earth. All arthropods have legs that bend. Insects, crabs, and spiders are arthropods.

A lot of legs!

Insects are arthropods with six legs. Spiders are arthropods with eight legs. There are even arthropods with more than one hundred legs!

A spider has eight legs. Each of its legs can bend.

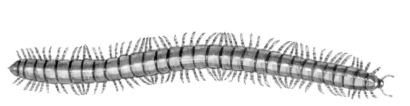

Some kinds of millipedes have more than one hundred legs!

A crab is an arthropod that has ten legs.

20

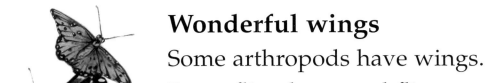

Wonderful wings

Some arthropods have wings. Butterflies, bees, and flies are arthropods that have wings. These arthropods use their wings to fly from place to place.

Many butterflies have colorful wings.

Many kinds of fish

Fish live in water. They are cold-blooded animals with backbones. Most fish have scales all over their bodies. Fish come in many shapes, colors, and sizes. Some fish are very small. Other fish are big. Some sharks are huge!

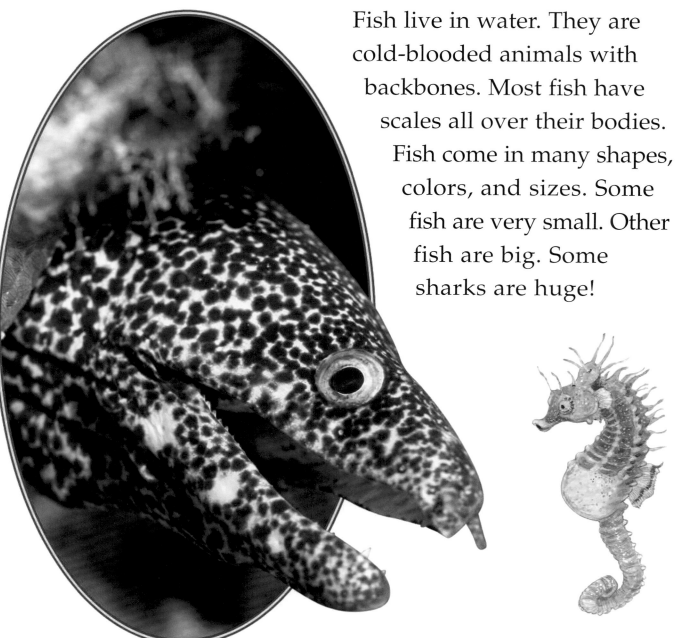

A moray eel is a fish that looks like a snake!

A sea horse may not look like a fish, but it is a fish!

Fish fins

Fish do not have legs for moving from place to place. Instead, they have **fins**. Fish use their fins to swim through water. Fins come in different shapes and sizes.

fins

fins

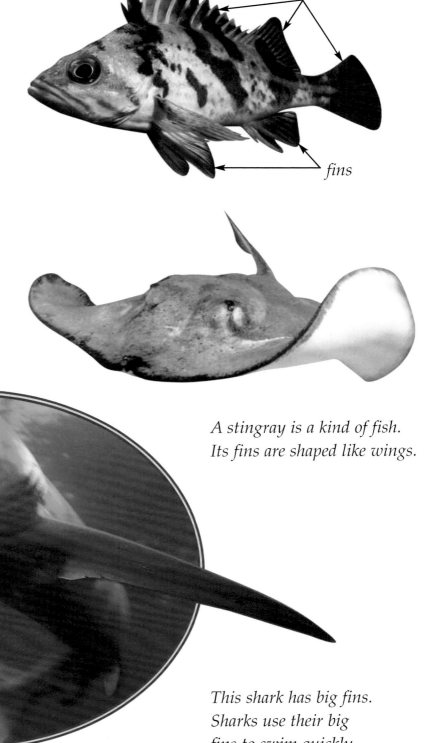

A stingray is a kind of fish. Its fins are shaped like wings.

This shark has big fins. Sharks use their big fins to swim quickly.

23

 # Amphibians

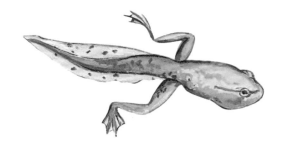

*A baby frog is called a **tadpole**. A tadpole lives in water. An adult frog lives on land.*

Frogs and toads are amphibians. Amphibians are animals that live in water and on land. When they are babies, amphibians live in water. When they are adults, amphibians live on land.

Toads and frogs

It is often hard to see the difference between a toad and a frog. A toad usually has bumpy, dry skin. A frog usually has smooth, wet skin. A toad has short back legs. A frog's back legs are longer.

The skin of this toad is covered with bumps.

salamander

newt

Amphibians with tails

Salamanders and newts are amphibians. These animals have tails. Frogs and toads do not have tails.

Reptiles

Turtles and lizards are two kinds of reptiles. Most reptiles have four legs, but some do not have any legs!

Some snakes are very long.

How big?

Some reptiles are small. A gecko is a small reptile. Other reptiles are big. Crocodiles and alligators are big, strong reptiles.

A lizard is a reptile. Like all reptiles, lizards are covered with scales.

Shells

Turtles and tortoises are reptiles. Turtles live mainly in water. Tortoises live on land. Both turtles and tortoises have shells. These animals move slowly on land because their shells are heavy.

A tortoise has strong legs to help it carry its heavy shell.

A sea turtle lives in water most of the time.

Beautiful birds

There are many kinds of birds on Earth. Some birds are big, and others are tiny. Birds are the only animals that are covered in feathers. Birds have two wings. Most birds can fly, but a few kinds of birds cannot fly.

These parrots have colorful feathers.

An ostrich has wings, but it cannot fly. It runs on its long, strong legs.

What a beak!

All birds have beaks. Beaks can be long and narrow or short and curved. Many birds use their beaks to build homes called **nests**. Birds also find food with their beaks. They then use their beaks to carry the food they find.

The crane is a bird that lives in water. It uses its long beak to catch fish.

*Baby birds are called **chicks**. These chicks have their beaks wide open. They are in their nest, waiting to be fed.*

The toucan uses its big beak to pick fruit from trees. It also uses its beak to catch insects and small reptiles to eat.

 # Mammals

Mammals are warm-blooded animals. All mammals have backbones. There are many kinds of mammals. Cats, dogs, horses, whales, and dolphins are mammals. People are mammals, too!

This boy and his cat are both mammals. You are also a mammal!

Some mammals live in water. Dolphins are mammals that live in water.

Mammal babies

Most mammal mothers take care of their babies. Mother mammals make milk inside their bodies to feed to their babies. Mammal babies drink milk for weeks or months. When the babies are old enough, their mothers teach them how to find food on their own.

Baby mammals look like their parents.

*Baby mammals **nurse**, or drink milk from the bodies of their mothers. These two baby tigers are nursing.*

Words to know and Index

amphibians
pages 4, 7, 10, 24-25

arthropods
pages 4, 6, 20-21

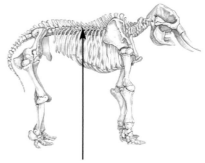

backbone
pages 8-9, 18, 22, 30

birds
pages 5, 6, 7,
11, 12, 15, 28-29

fish
pages 4, 6,
13, 22-23, 29

desert   *forest*

habitats
pages 12-13

mammals
pages 5, 7, 11, 30-31

mollusks
pages 4, 6, 9, 18-19

reptiles
pages 5, 6, 10, 26-27, 29

worms
pages 4, 17